Power Endurance

Fatigue Management for Rock Climbing

STEVE BECHTEL, CSCS

CONTENTS

CLIMB STRONG

ACKNOWLEDGMENTS

Many thanks to my wife, Ellen, and our wonderful staff at Elemental Performance + Fitness for making a great environment in which to train and learn. Thanks also to the great climber Steve Petro for starting me down this path. Finally, thanks to my good friend Sylvia Carl for reviewing these notes and helping progress the Climb Strong program.

Fatigue Management for Rock Climbing

Power Endurance is a terrible term, but when it comes to climbing, no one mistakes its meaning. It's the ugly world between bouldering and "normal" route climbing, where there is no rest, a heart rate that's quickly maxing out, and all you can do is make a desperate sprint for the chains. It's painful, frequently ugly, and the least fun to train for. That's where effective *fatigue management* training comes in.

The best way to train for fatigue management is by doing intervals. Interval training, hard bouts of effort interspersed with short rest periods, is an excellent tool for developing improved endurance and "power endurance" in climbers. By breaking up high-intensity efforts, we can accomplish more work in a given amount of time and condition the body to deal with inadequate recovery, a situation faced frequently in climbing. We do intervals in climbing training in order to better perform hard moves in a state of fatigue while also allowing a decreased sense of fatigue at any given level.

I've put together this book as a general reference guide to varying methods of training one might use to improve climbing fatigue management, whether you call it work capacity, strength-endurance, power-endurance, recovery, or stamina. This is not a collection of workouts. It is a tool designed to be used within the confines of a well-planned training cycle. The sessions suggested in this book are entirely dependent on progressions, using the stress and recovery from one workout to enhance the value of subsequent workouts. Randomly "throwing in" a 4x4 workout is worse than a waste of time. Physiological adaptation is dependent on repeated overloads that are similar enough in nature to stimulate the body to adapt.

The best term for the realm between the strength-related demands of bouldering and the fitness required for routes is really **strength-endurance**. The definition of this term is *the ability to create continued muscular tension for extended periods without a decrease in efficiency*. Sounds about right to me. Over the past twenty years or so, however, rock climbers have come to call this power-endurance instead. Although in scientific terms these are not synonyms, it's hard to separate the two in the real worlds of rock climbing. I hate the term power endurance, but we need to speak the same language.

It is my firm belief that interval-style training is the best way for climbers to apply their bouldering strength to the demands of route climbing. This book is designed to help get you there.

A Few Notes on Training in General

Early on in a climbing career, almost any form of exercise or climbing can lead to improvement. As a climber's *training age* increases, though, demands placed on the system during training must be more and more specific in order for the athlete to develop. Eventually total training volume becomes limited, both by ability to recover and time available to train. For these reasons, an advanced climber's training requires more intense work, technical refinement, and higher-quality efforts in training. Bottom line: train harder, not longer.

Climbing is an extraordinarily complex sport and should be treated as such. Reductionist thinking, applying simple models to complex systems, must be avoided. Thus training strength, power, and endurance, in their traditional athletic sense, becomes impossible. Every single thing we do in climbing requires use of the very ends of the kinetic chain (fingers and toes), where our ability to apply force is severely limited. Add to this that the body is under constant tension for the duration of a route or problem, and it becomes difficult to apply the rules of triathlon, bodybuilding, or almost any other sport to climbing. One of the most important things a climber can do is to spend large periods of time *practicing* climbing and focusing on different aspects of the sport. After the first few months, most of us quit practicing climbing and simply move in and out of condition while

4

maintaining a fixed ability level, leaving critical skills underdeveloped.

The only unalterable requirement in climbing improvement is to develop basic strength enough to do hard moves, and the extension of distance over which these moves can be executed. That is what we do with bouldering and, later, with interval training. I argue that "just climbing" is not enough. I've heard all the examples of this or that guy that spends his life at the crag and always climbs well. The examples are anomalies. The examples are not you.

Novice, Intermediate, and Advanced Athletes

In the early stages of climbing, almost anything will cause a climber to get better. At this level, simply adding any kind of climbing or even general physical activity is the best path to improvement. "Training" is a waste of time for climbers at this level; their climbing should be looked at as practice and measured only in hours. Anyone who has not put in at least one to two thousand hours (and by this I mean actual hours of movement - not hours spent at the crag or gym) in the sport is still a novice when it comes to training age.

An intermediate-level climber begins to really know failure (and the desire to succeed) on routes and problems. Bouldering, hangboard sessions, and disorganized "training" can be employed to help this climber improve. Usually, by the time a climber has reached this level, he is already at 60-80% of his genetic potential for strength and endurance. Progress really flattens out for the intermediate and these climbers will often hit a long-term plateau; the result of progress simply taking too much work. Many climbers will never leave this plateau, a place business guru Seth Godin describes as "the dip." The intermediate stage can last several years and will take a climber to around 90% of his genetic potential.

Advanced climbers are rare. These are the ones who continually creep up the improvement ladder, even years into a training career. They follow structured plans, and expect to perform at top levels only a few short weeks each year. These climbers are generally well-rounded, and don't have a particular "style." Efficiency decreases stress. The better you are, the harder you must train.

Strength coach Mark Rippetoe describes the advanced (Weightlifting) trainee well:
"Advanced trainees are very close to their genetic potential. Huge amounts of training result in relatively small improvements. Advanced trainees require fewer movements than intermediates.
Advanced trainees require large volumes of intense work to disrupt homeostasis. This means the stress required for progress will creep nearer and nearer to the maximal tolerable workload that the body can perform and recover from."

Don't be deceived. There are climbers performing at very high levels that have not reached the advanced stage; they simply have more potential that they have not tapped. Likewise, there are climbers that might climb only 5.11 that have attained advanced status simply because they are performing very close to their absolute genetic limit.

Random training is never superior to planned training. Understand that there is no incidence in human learning or progression where this rule does not apply. Not even in a CrossFit gym. We stray toward random workouts because they are more interesting and because doing something random is quite easy; there is no set bar for what needs to be done in the session. Random workouts might work well for novices, but it is a path to staleness and injury for more advanced athletes.

"If you want pain, learn Muai Thai. If you want to learn about failure, play golf. If you want to vomit, drink syrup of epicac. If you want to become stronger and more fit, train appropriately."
– Brian Petty

A note on volume
Training volume (total time climbing) does not have a clear relationship with performance. What I mean by this is that even though one climber might climb twice as much as another, he won't necessarily be better. Conversely, the climber that consistently tries harder problems and routes, generally the one you see falling at the crag, will almost always be the better redpoint climber. Once you've reached your optimum training volume for a given period, intensity is the only way forward.

Other training
Aerobic training should be done as little as possible. Scientific evidence clearly shows that the development of strength, power, and speed are adversely affected

by steady-state aerobic training. Aerobic capacity should instead be developed as a by-product of anaerobic training and of regular climbing. Research into the use of steady-state endurance training for strength and power athletes strongly suggests that this type of training interferes with *all* the parameters such athletes are concerned with developing.

With that in mind, "ARC" training (aerobic restoration and capillarity) is probably not a good way to improve top-end performance. Too much low-intensity training forces a fundamental compromise at a cellular level. ARC training may very well increase blood flow to muscles and will undoubtedly facilitate faster recovery. But are we enhancing the recovery ability of an athlete we've made weaker?

In climbing, endurance represents the ability to produce many consecutive bursts of anaerobic or near-anaerobic effort. Such endurance is best produced by increasing the number of intense bouts of hard movement, rather than by increasing the volume of easy, aerobically driven moves, since this more closely duplicates the metabolic demands of sport.

The one defense of ARC that I'll accept is this: technique is better developed in a state of low fatigue. By consistently climbing with improving movement in mind, these sessions can be quite useful. "Junk" training, just climbing around the gym on open holds, however, is probably doing more harm than good for climbers who need to develop technique and strength.

Core training
Stop the sit-ups! The requirements of hard climbing
don't include sitting on your ass and drawing your
chest toward your knees. What a climber needs is
"core strength," which really means the *prevention of
motion;* connecting the human kinetic chain. What
you're trying to do by training the core is to coordinate
the action of the limbs via the torso while preventing
energy leaks - areas where power is lost due to sloppy
movement or sagging. This kind of training is well
integrated with intervals, whether before, after, or
during sessions.

All core training exercises for climbers need to
fall into four categories:

Anti-Rotation - Preventing the torso from
rotating under load. Secondarily, we can train
rotation, where we rotate under load.

Stability - Plank-type, static hold exercises.

Dynamic Stability - Movement of one limb or a
pair of limbs while holding a static position.

Torso / Hip Flexion - Movement at the hip or
shoulders with the upper limbs fixed.

Why Interval Training?

Since the mid-twentieth century, top athletes in many sports have used interval training as a means of achieving higher performance. Our primary goals when using this form of training are to optimize *strength-endurance* (SE) and, more generally, *work capacity* (WC). We throw around plenty of terms for the same thing, when we all mean *fatigue management*. Whether it's strength-endurance, power-endurance, anaerobic endurance, or muscular endurance, it's all about performing better under fatigue.

Interval climbing-based workouts are a specific and effective way of managing fatigue. Running, weight training, and even alpine climbing pale in comparison when it comes to building the stamina to try hard routes all day long. Specificity is so important to performance climbing that it almost doesn't matter what kind of climbing you're doing - any climbing is probably better than the best weight training or cross training program. Most climbers that train with weight run into problems when they assign too much importance to those workouts.

We use several methods for developing this work capacity in climbers at our facility. In general, these methods fall into 4 categories:

- High-Volume (Continuous Work) Efforts: This includes all forms of steady-state training, alpine climbing, long days at the crags, etc.
- Cross-Training Methods: This category includes "climbing specific" resistance training, general resistance training, and doing other sports.
- Density Training: This is the active addition of more work in a given work period. I'll cover this in detail later.
- Climbing Intervals (including Route Repetitions): This is the primary focus of this text.

More frequent practice results in better skill acquisition. Therefore, instead of hammering out long hours on the climbing wall until you can't lift your arms, train more often, but for less time. **Skill acquisition slows with the accumulation of fatigue.** In fact, if an athlete becomes too fatigued in training, he starts to use poor form, resulting in a degradation of skill and an increase in potential for injury.

When training for strength, power, or technical improvement, failure is an integral part of the formula. In training for strength endurance, technical correctness is paramount, and climbing problems without failing is an important factor in overloading the system correctly. Failure in these workouts will result from built-up fatigue, while failure bouldering or on a systems wall typically comes from an inability to do the moves. The value of intervals is compromised when you can no longer use good technique.

Specificity is critical. Hold size, wall angle, distance between holds, and several other factors should be considered. Having a high level of endurance on big holds and steep rock does not necessarily translate to endurance on small edges.

There are 4 physiological variables to manipulate in any interval program:
>   duration (distance) of interval
>   intensity of movement
>   duration of rest periods
>   number of repetitions

We build our interval problems in three mostly-arbitrary lengths. These are short (1-4 moves), medium (5-20 moves) and long (20+ moves). These (very) roughly coincide with the energy systems the body uses to deliver fuel during exercise, not really because of the number of moves of climbing one does, but because of the amount of time the body is under stress (and the intensity of that stress) each set.

Fatigue resistance workouts need only be done 1-3 times per week leading up to a heavy redpoint period, and then can drop to once a week for about 4-5 weeks while you "peak." The longer your build-up to redpointing, the longer it'll last. Usually, my plans call for about 4-6 weeks of this training (in addition to bouldering and strength work), but you can see results with as few as 2 weeks' work, or 3-6 sessions. That being said, intervals are appropriate in other training phases, as well. Intervals are integral to our standard non-linear plans and our alternating-linear plans, too. More on this in the planning section of this handbook.

Getting "ridiculously pumped" is never the goal of true endurance training. Understand that building a massive pump at the end of a session or climbing day does not lead to greater endurance. In order to stimulate the system to improve endurance and recovery capacity, we must stay close to an athlete's anaerobic threshold - a place where efficient and effective movement is still possible. It's here that the greatest volume of useful exercise can take place. Too far from here, either more or less intense, and results are compromised.

How to know where this is? Short of taking blood during a training session, it's hard to pinpoint. Additionally, it's not just blood lactate that causes fatigue in climbers; both the muscular endurance and strength of the of the forearm play crucial roles. The best we can do is to stay close to this level by working up to a fatigue state, then backing off. If you fall due to too much fatigue or pump, you're doing more damage than good. Conversely, if your training doesn't cause fatigue and some loss in grip strength toward the end of the session, you're probably not trying hard enough.

The majority of the climbing interval workouts are best performed on a climbing wall, though some of the exercises are more appropriate for a system wall or actual rock climbs. Although I think it will be obvious, I will try to note these differences.

Of special note is the problem with judging intensity of boulder problems based on their grade. Problems can be overgraded, undergraded, suit your strengths, be tweaky, or can be inconsistent. With this in mind, I recommend doing one or two of the following interval workouts throughout an entire training phase, using the **exact same problems** for each similar workout. By doing the same problems in series of sessions, you can get a more accurate feel for progress and intensity. I'll note specifics within the context of each workout.

I'll state again that a detailed training log is critical. Training logs should include the day's goal, the training phase goal, how each and every workout felt, the duration, intensity, and your bodyweight for that session. Nutrition can also be logged.

The Interval Workouts

Hard Repetitions
PURPOSE: To top-out maximum anaerobic levels
TYPE OF CLIMB OR PROBLEM: short, hard, sustained
NUMBER OF MOVES: 3-8
DURATION (APPROXIMATE): 15 seconds
WORK-TO-REST RATIO: up to 1:10
DIFFICULTY: OS +1 to OS +3
NUMBER OF REPEATS PER SESSION: 8-15

Hard repetitions are repeated difficult boulder problems done with a fixed rest period between. These intervals are used to top out a climber's maximum strength-endurance levels, as he'll be doing fairly hard moves throughout the workout. Problems should be short (3-8 moves) and fairly sustained; stay away from problems with distinct crux moves.

Total work time for each problem should be under 15 seconds. If selecting problems in a gym makes this impossible, simply pick a spot to end the problem where it suits the workout, regardless of where the problem officially ends.

For this workout, you'll want to pick two or three problems that are at 1-3 V-grades above your onsight level. Repeating these problems in sequence, you'll do three to five circuits, ultimately completing 8-15 total problems.

Progression in these intervals is usually managed by decreasing the rest periods between problems rather than increasing the difficulty of the problems. This is simply because finding suitable problems workout-to-workout can be challenging. Even though a problem might be technically harder, it's not always a better choice for training.

POWER
ENDURANCE

Again you've got to keep in mind that the goal of the session is to improve metabolic pathways and muscular endurance, not to complete limit-level problems.

Easy Intervals

PURPOSE: To build base fitness, work on basic skills
TYPE OF CLIMB OR PROBLEM: very easy problems on a variety of terrain
NUMBER OF MOVES: 8-15
DURATION (APPROXIMATE): 10-30 seconds
WORK-TO-REST RATIO: 1:1 to 1:3
DIFFICULTY: Warm-Up
NUMBER OF REPEATS PER SESSION: 30 (6 sets of 5)

Easy Intervals aren't exactly easy, it's just that you'll use easy problems to do them. These intervals are done to help build work capacity in climbers, and to develop good movement skills under slight fatigue.

The standard workout format for these intervals is to do 5 repeats of one problem (or 5 similar problems), then rest for a period equal to your work time. Repeat the same sequence of problems (with equal rest) again two more times. After the third interval, rest 10-15 minutes, then repeat the sequence again for three more intervals.

I recommend using a variety of problems on different angles and hold-types. Avoid using problems that are too difficult - you should only feel a minor pump after the first few intervals. If you get to the halfway rest and feel whooped, your problems are too hard.

Short Intervals

PURPOSE: Increase anaerobic threshold, improve speed of recovery
TYPE OF CLIMB OR PROBLEM: 5 separate sustained problems
NUMBER OF MOVES: 6-12
DURATION (APPROXIMATE): 5-20 seconds
WORK-TO-REST RATIO: 1:2 to 1:5
DIFFICULTY: OS
NUMBER OF REPEATS PER SESSION: 15 (3 sets of 5)

In the short interval workout, the climber does five problems at around his onsight limit separated by 2-3 minutes each. After completing all five problems, a 10-15 minute rest is taken. After the rest, the entire sequence is repeated two more times, for a total of 15 problems.

To advance this workout, you're going to want to think about what you want to get out of them. If doing harder moves under fatigue, such as short sprint-style routes, is your goal, plan to select more difficult problems in the next workout following successful completion of a workout. If building longer-term endurance or recovery ability is the goal, try to keep the difficulty of the problems the same workout-to-workout, but decrease the rest between problems by about 15-20 seconds.

It's best not to decrease the 10-15 minute period between groups, however. This tends to lead toward diminished quality of effort, especially by the third round. This, in turn, leads to a less effective workout overall.

Boulder Problem Blocks (4x4s, etc.)

PURPOSE: To build extended power endurance and strength endurance, increase anaerobic capacity
TYPE OF CLIMB OR PROBLEM: A fixed number (3-7) of problems
NUMBER OF MOVES: 5-15
DURATION (APPROXIMATE): 10-20 seconds each prob, 2-5 minutes per set
WORK-TO-REST RATIO: none between problems, 4-12 min between sets
DIFFICULTY: OS-2 to OS+2
NUMBER OF REPEATS PER SESSION: 3-6 sets

Probably the most popular interval-style training in climbing is the boulder problem block, and probably the most popular block is the 4x4. Boulder Problem Blocks (BPBs) are very easy to implement in a normal bouldering gym and allow for very effective strength endurance workouts. A normal workout consists of 3 to 7 problems done back-to-back, and then repeated for 3 to 6 sets. As a general rule, the more problems you do, the fewer sets you'd be able to effectively complete.

A traditional 4x4 workout consists of four similar problems (or problems specific to your training objectives) done back-to-back, then repeated three more times in the same sequence. A rest of 4+ minutes is taken between each set. After completing all four sets, the climber then rests 15-25 minutes, and does another complete 4x4 group. The second group is often completed using slightly easier problems. Remember - quality of movement is paramount and sloppy technique does not serve the end purpose of becoming a better climber.

We typically do three different types of BPBs:

4x4s - 2 groups of 4 problems done 4 times each, with 15-25 minutes between groups.
6x3s - 2 groups of 3 problems done 6 times each, with 15-25 minutes between groups.
4x7s - 1 group of 7 problems done 4 times, with about 10 minutes between groups.

You can also adjust the intensity of these efforts by careful selection of the problems used. A "normal" workout uses problems of a consistent grade. An ascending set, for example, doing a v3-v5-v5-v6 progression, can be used for longer power-endurance benefits. Descending sets, such as v7-v5-v4-v4 are better for more sustained routes with easier moves. Alternating sets, such as v3-v6-v3-v6 are valid, and bridge the gap between ascending and descending intervals.

I reiterate that consistency is key. The best way to gauge progress is to do an entire training cycle using the same workout format, logging the problems carefully and addressing specific needs.

CLIMB
STRONG

Timed Repeats
PURPOSE: Developing maximum anaerobic power
TYPE OF CLIMB OR PROBLEM: 2-3 short problems that require
powerful movement
NUMBER OF MOVES: 3-10
DURATION (APPROXIMATE): 30-45 seconds per problem (trying for
about half the duration of each time cycle)
WORK-TO-REST RATIO: 1:1
DIFFICULTY: OS-3 to OS
NUMBER OF REPEATS PER SESSION: 20, separated into 2 groups of
10

In timed repeats, we combine both work and recovery into a fixed time period. For example, you might do one boulder problem per minute for 10 minutes. The faster you complete the problem, the more recovery you get. By necessity, easier problems must be programmed into this workout, as recovery is limited to about a 1:1 ratio. The fatigue caused by this workout is unbelievable.

We program 2-3 problems of similar difficulty, to be alternated throughout the work time. Doing just one problem gets tedious, trying to do too many degrades the quality of the work completed. Most of the time, we keep it simple and go for 1 minute repeats. As a variation, a 90 second count or a 2 minute count can be implemented. Both of the latter variations are less intense than minute repeats. An interval timer is pretty handy for these workouts. Many watches are equipped with them these days, or you might like the Gym Boss, a dedicated interval timer for around $20.

Long Intervals

PURPOSE: To build route-specific anaerobic endurance and strength endurance
TYPE OF CLIMB OR PROBLEM: Long problems or pairs of problems that are sustained in nature
NUMBER OF MOVES: 15-30
DURATION (APPROXIMATE): 30-90 seconds
WORK-TO-REST RATIO: 1:1 to 1:4
DIFFICULTY: OS-3 to OS-1
NUMBER OF REPEATS PER SESSION: 8-12

Long intervals are usually a staple of our redpoint-phase training. We use them to pull our 10-12 move strength-endurance efforts into usable route endurance. In this workout, we like to repeat a single problem or traverse five times in a row with 2-3 minutes between. After a series of 5, rest 10+ minutes, and then do the same sequence of 5 again. Intensity should be such that you can just complete the tenth problem.

This workout is more about sustaining medium to hard efforts than doing hard moves. If you select problems that are too difficult, you'll fail to see the benefits this training has to offer.

As a less-strict variation, we've occasionally done "song intervals" where a climber moves continuously for the (wildly variable) duration of one song, then rests for the duration of the next song. To avoid dumbing down the climbing, we try to stick to actual problems or marked traverses rather than "open climbing," where one's movement quality and footwork are compromised.

Route Laps

PURPOSE: Developing route-specific muscular endurance and metabolic pathways
TYPE OF CLIMB OR PROBLEM: Done on actual sustained climbs, avoiding rest positions
NUMBER OF MOVES: 15-50
DURATION (APPROXIMATE): 30 seconds to 5 minutes
WORK-TO-REST RATIO:1:1 to 1:3
DIFFICULTY: OS-3 to OS+1
NUMBER OF REPEATS PER SESSION: 4 to 12

We do these at the crag. This is probably the best single way to train route-specific stamina. It takes a patient climbing partner, or a high-level of skill with solo-belay techniques. Pick a route or two, and climb. Try to start out with a rest period equal to twice your climbing duration, then whittle the rest down until the ratio is 1:1. A good practice is to stop the workout when you fall off due to fatigue. A minor slip due to error is OK.

Whether to toprope or lead these routes is controversial. Toproping allows for quicker movement, convenience, and a bit more calm for some climbers. (a side note: If fear is an issue of any sort for you, this training is probably a waste of time.) By leading the routes, on the other hand, a climber gets a more specific training stimulus, and operates at a higher arousal level.

Recovery Intervals

PURPOSE: Building the ability to recover in "active" positions
TYPE OF CLIMB OR PROBLEM: A traverse or climb with 2-3 rest positions
NUMBER OF MOVES: 15-40
DURATION (APPROXIMATE): 4-8 minutes per lap
WORK-TO-REST RATIO: 1:1 or 1:2 (active)
DIFFICULTY: OS-3 to OS
NUMBER OF REPEATS PER SESSION: 4-6

In recovery intervals, we work on building the ability to get something back at a rest stance. Many of today's hard routes feature short crux sequences separated by relatively good stances where a fit climber can recover. Although recovery is primarily enhanced by active climbing, there is great skill in calming the system enough to get some "clean blood" back into the muscles.

To set up good recovery laps, pick a problem or traverse that has 2-3 good rest stances on it, ideally at the beginning, middle and end of the problem. To begin, step off the ground and immediately hang out and rest 30 seconds. Next, climb through the problem to half way, rest 30 seconds, then continue to the end, and then recover at the finish hold for about 30 seconds. Climb back to the mid-point rest, then do the same. Continue back to the start hold, and take a third 30 second rest. At this point you can stop the interval, or can add a second lap to the effort. The determining factor is really what kind of climbing you're attempting to improve.

To progress these intervals, increasing active rest time doesn't really make sense. The better method for making these work for you is to either make the recovery stances more strenuous or to make the climbing between stances more difficult. Again, it depends on what you're going for.

A wonderful example of taking recovery very seriously was my friend Frank Dusl's training in the early 1990s. He had a training routine that consisted of routinely doing a long problem and then removing the most-restful stance. I wrote about it a few years back in an article called "Another Way to Endure."

Endurance training comes in many forms and it can be argued (weakly) that any climbing you do that makes you tired makes you better at enduring fatigue. As I've said before, most climbers who boulder indoors are, in fact, training endurance when they think they're training power. Problem is, they are training an ability to boulder for hours rather than the ability to hang with it on routes. This kind of training is not wrong if you want to boulder for hours...

My personal experience and that of many other climbers is that interval training is the best way to top-end endurance. This is not the only way, though. One of the best endurance training workouts I've ever seen was developed in the 1990s by Frank Dusl. This is the workout that resulted in his now famous quote: "I don't get pumped anymore, I just lose a little contact strength."

He was, and still is as far as I know, a master of discipline. Most of his climbing sessions were on his 12' x 12' home wall, a flat plane that overhung about 30 degrees. The wall was covered in holds of all shapes and sizes, and he had a numbered "route" that criss-crossed the wall many times, consisting of over 50 moves. He tried this route, probably 5.13 of some kind, until he could do it one way, then worked it again until he could reverse it. Then he linked it...over a hundred moves.

POWER
ENDURANCE

*Then, and this is the genius, he took off the best hold
and replaced it with a crappy little one. He then
worked it until he could climb it again, and then
removed the best hold again. He did this again and
again over the following months. Our friend Todd
Skinner tried the problem at this point and declared it
"5.14 something" to do just one-way. The thing was,
Frank could now do the route two to three times
without stepping off the wall. We're talking twenty-plus
minutes of hard moves with very little rest.*

*Like a mad scientist in his lab, Frank removed himself
from the mainstream of training and asked himself the
fundamental questions. What he came up with was
genius and madness combined. What he built was one
of the best climbers America has never seen.*

Linked Problems

PURPOSE: Enhancing the ability to climb long sections of strength-endurance
TYPE OF CLIMB OR PROBLEM: 2-4 problems in close proximity
NUMBER OF MOVES: 5-12 moves per problem
DURATION (APPROXIMATE): 2-5 minutes
WORK-TO-REST RATIO: 1:3
DIFFICULTY: OS to OS+3
NUMBER OF REPEATS PER SESSION: 4-6

Linked problems are simply 2-4 problems done back-to-back, downclimbing between each rather than stepping off the wall. The problems we'll use are often referred to as "up-down-ups," but we tend to complicate things a bit and the notation gets cumbersome. The exercises are as follows:

- N problems - Up, down, then up again, just like writing the letter "N." Two problems linked by a downclimb. Also called a 2-link.

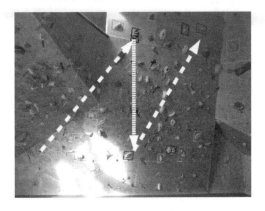

- M I problems - 3 problems linked by downclimbs (up-down-up-down-up). Also called a 3-link.

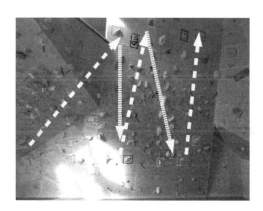

- M N problems - Up, down, up, down, up, down, up. (4 problems linked by downclimbs.) Also called a 4-link.

- T 2 P - A traverse into a problem, usually an easier traverse to a near-limit problem.

The most important part of these intervals is to climb in a state of fatigue. Select problems that are very close to your limit, and try to make sure that you BARELY hit the last holds of the final climb. Naturally, you'll want to climb on a variety of angles and hold types, but should aim toward problems that simulate your goal routes; Smith Rocks climbers should stay out of the bouldering cave.

As opposed to a standard 4x4 or other BPB, you should seek pretty full recovery between intervals, the standard is resting 3 times as long as you climbed.

POWER
ENDURANCE

A typical 4 week progression looks like this:
Week One Session One (W1S1): 4 x N with 5 min between.
W1S2: 2 x N, 2 x MI with 5-8 min between.
W2S1: 2 x N, 3 x MI with 5-8 min between.
W2S2: 2 x N, 4 x MI with 5-8 min between.
W3S1: 4 x MI, 1 x MN with 8-10 min between.
W3S2: 4 x MI, 2 x MN with 8-10 min between.
W4S1: 3 x MI, 3 x MN with 8-10 min between.
W4S2: 2 x MI, 4 x MN with 8-10 min between.

Naturally, your problem selection and duration should reflect your goals. If you're climbing in the Frankenjura, you're doing shorter, more powerful routes and probably don't need too much easier volume. If you're training for 5.12 at the Red, you can skip the hard moves, work on doing several MNs of easier problems in a session, and spend more time with recovery intervals.

No-Stopping Sets

PURPOSE: Maximizing power endurance and strength endurance
TYPE OF CLIMB OR PROBLEM: A long traverse or 2-3 linkable problems
NUMBER OF MOVES: 15-30
DURATION (APPROXIMATE): 2-4 minutes
WORK-TO-REST RATIO: 1:3 to 1:5
DIFFICULTY: OS-1 to OS+1
NUMBER OF REPEATS PER SESSION: 4-6

The essence, and perhaps beauty, of a continuously strenuous route is that there is just no way to recover. We use many different names for this, but power-endurance is the best known. In a no-stopping set, you have to consciously climb a series of hard moves without the typical stop-and-rest style most of us use. Whether you can stop or not on the problems you choose for this workout, you've got to stomp between moves as if the clock were ticking.

It's best to set a series of problems that requires this style of movement, but this is easier said than done. Instead, a creative climber will step off the ground and force himself to start moving quickly and decisively between holds. By the end of a given set, the climber is usually breathing hard and is pretty pumped. Make sure the problems are easy enough you can actually do them in this swifter style. It takes some getting used to.

Rhythm Intervals

PURPOSE: Developing forearm strength endurance
TYPE OF CLIMB OR PROBLEM: 4 matched holds in a grid and a rest jug
NUMBER OF MOVES: n/a
DURATION (APPROXIMATE): 4 minutes per set
WORK-TO-REST RATIO:1:1
DIFFICULTY: n/a
NUMBER OF REPEATS PER SESSION: 2 to 3

The basic set up is like this: Get two sets of 4 matching holds, preferably a set of large edges and a set of slopers or cobbles. Set both groups of these up with two about shoulder-width apart and the other two about 2-2.5 feet above, also at shoulder-width apart. In the middle, about halfway between the holds, place a nice big rest jug (imagine making an X with the holds, this would be at the center.)
On the wall below your interval holds, place enough foot holds to avoid having to think about footwork - this is a forearm-only workout.
The workout goes like this:
Set a timer to chime every 30 seconds. Get on the wall using the large edges and start your clock. Move your left hand up to the higher edge, then back down, right hand up, then back down. Repeat this slowly and deliberately (usually we'll see 4-6 moves per hand in 30 seconds) until the timer beeps. At this point, switch to your rest jug and shake out for 30 seconds. Repeat this sequence three more times, for a total of 4 minutes.
After this first 4 minute bout, rest passively (on the ground) for 4 minutes, followed by another 4 minute work bout on the other set of holds.

Mei Ratz photo

You can make this harder as you improve by:
-Making the holds smaller (if you need to improve endurance on small holds).
-Spacing the holds further apart (if reaching / locking off is a weakness).
-Decreasing the size of the rest hold (if your climbing area doesn't provide many rest jugs).
-Increasing the work time to 5 rounds rather than 4.
(And so on, as your particular circumstances require.)
This is easy to tag on to a regular bouldering session, at the end of another interval/endurance workout, or best of all, alongside a hangboard workout.

Density Training

PURPOSE: Developing maximum anaerobic power and strength endurance
TYPE OF CLIMB OR PROBLEM: 3-4 short problems that are continuous in nature
NUMBER OF MOVES: 3-10
DURATION (APPROXIMATE): 20 minutes per group, 60 minutes per session
WORK-TO-REST RATIO: as needed
DIFFICULTY: OS to OS+2
NUMBER OF REPEATS PER SESSION: varies

Density training isn't exactly interval training, but it's so utterly effective, I had to put it in this book.

Here's the basic set-up: Pick 3-4 problems at your onsight level or just a bit above. You can choose these to simulate a specific route you're trying or you can choose a few different styles if you're training for onsighting/general fitness. You're going to set a clock for 20 minutes, and start climbing through problems 1-4 as quickly as your muscles will allow. Rest as needed between problems, but keep track of the total number of successful sends you get.

Most climbers will be able to get 10 or more problems the first time. You're going to want to rest about 20 minutes after the first bout, then hit another 20 minutes of density-either on the same 4 problems or 4 new ones. The big key to this workout is repeating it. You'll see the best results if you do it 2 or 3 times per week for 3-5 weeks. By the end, you should be hitting close to 20 problems each set. Most of our athletes improve by 50-75% each time we roll through a 4 - week block.

1-2-3-4

PURPOSE: Developing endurance across a broad spectrum
TYPE OF CLIMB OR PROBLEM: Several problems or a long traverse
NUMBER OF MOVES: varies
DURATION (APPROXIMATE): varies
WORK-TO-REST RATIO: recover to 60% MHR, or 1:1
DIFFICULTY: OS-3 to OS
NUMBER OF REPEATS PER SESSION: 2

1-2-3-4 is a progression of greater climbing duration each time, while recovering either to a fixed heart rate (60% of predicted maximum) or simply a 1:1 work:rest. Get warm, set a clock, and climb a minute without rests or easy stances. Again, following problems or marked traverses is superior to climbing "open." Rest either a minute or until you recover to 60%, then climb for 2 minutes. Repeat for 3 and then 4 minutes, then take a rest for about 10 minutes. When you've recovered fully, repeat the sequence again.

Avoiding too much time "open" climbing is a good idea. No matter how careful we think we're being, the climbing inevitably falls into patterns of movement that we've got mastered. Keep this in mind when building your programs.

Additional Notes on Training

Adding a bouldering (short) workout each week provides enough intensity that neuromuscular function is reinforced without fatally upping the volume. It is my opinion that a climber should boulder year-round, since the strength and power requirements of climbing are almost always present.

The concept of *adaptation persistence* plays a crucial role in performance preparation for some sports. In order, here are the most persistent to least persistent facets of performance:

hypertrophy
strength
muscular endurance
power
technique
cardiovascular endurance

The most persistent factors should be planned earliest in the training cycle, furthest from performance.

The campus board is the bench press of a climbing gym; it's where guys that don't really know how to get *better* go to look *strong*. Campusing is inappropriate for 95% of climbers who do it. The chance of injury is very high, and the true performance gains to be made are slight. Furthermore, most people do it for the wrong reasons. It is highly unlikely that accuracy and contact strength are your real weaknesses. Unless your technique is perfect, there are better places to spend you training time than on this device.

Don't climb sub-maximal routes like they're hard for you. If they are easy, climb them like they are easy. This habit can then be tried on harder routes. The more casual you "act" the more your body will relax and perform well.

Climbing slowly is neurologically different than climbing explosively. Climbing explosively is what we do at the top end of our ability. Therefore, climbing slowly does not train us well for maximum performance.

Training Plans

Training plans and programs are where the real difference is made. The plan need not be complicated nor particularly elegant, but it must be followed. More times than I can count, I've seen climbers put together a great training plan and fail to follow it. The solution? Start simple. Set up a plan that you can execute, execute it, and complicate it in the next cycle if you must.

Below I have laid out three different training plan templates that have been effective for improving performance in climbers I have trained. I have selected these because they are designed with an improvement in strength endurance in mind. Note, however, that these are not purely interval training plans.

Program 1: Alternating Linear (7-9 weeks, repeatable.)

I started using this plan with my climbers that couldn't stick with a plan. Then I started using it myself. Now, I think it might be the best general plan for most of us. This plan is based on some basic research into adaptation, showing:

- That repeated overload with similar stressors causes adaptation.
- That adaptation to most stressors plateaus after 3-4 weeks.
- That exposure to too many stressors suppresses adaptation.

Are you ready? The simplest (effective) training plan I could come up with goes like this: Train three weeks of intensity-focused bouldering, followed by three weeks of volume-focused strength-endurance climbing. Repeat.
The bouldering is progressed by adding harder problems or more, hard problems with each training session. The strength-endurance (interval focus) is progressed by adding more total medium-difficulty mileage to a fixed time-frame. This is represented by a simple formula: number of problems (or links) x difficulty of problems / minutes in workout. This number should increase slightly each workout for all 3 weeks before switching back to intensity-focused training.
Example:

POWER
ENDURANCE

Intensity Phase:
Workout 1: V4 V5 V5 V4 V5 V4 V6 V4 V5 (total v-sum: 42, avg. difficulty: 4.5)
Workout 2: V5 V5 V5 V4 V5 V4 V6 V4 V6 (total v-sum: 44, avg. difficulty: 4.9)
Workout 3: V5 V6 V5 V4 V5 V4 V6 V4 V5 V6 (total v-sum: 50, avg. difficulty: 5.0)
Workout 4: V5 V6 V5 V4 V6 V4 V6 V4 V5 V6 (total v-sum: 51, avg. difficulty: 5.1)
Workout 5: V5 V6 V7 V4 V5 V4 V6 V4 V5 V7 (total v-sum: 53, avg. difficulty: 5.3)
Workout 6: V6 V6 V5 V5 V6 V7 V6 V7 (total v-sum: 48, avg. difficulty: 5.3)
Workout 7: V6 V6 V5 V5 V6 V7 V6 V7 V6 (total v-sum: 54, avg. difficulty: 5.4)

Strength-Endurance Phase (using 2 sets of 4x4s) :

Workout 1: V3-V3-V4-V4 / V3-V3-V4-V4 (48 minutes). Total difficulty (28/48)=.583
Workout 2: V3-V4-V4-V4 / V3-V4-V4-V4 (46 minutes). Total difficulty (30/46)=.652
Workout 3: V3-V4-V4-V4 / V3-V4-V4-V4 (44 minutes). Total difficulty (30/44)=.681
Workout 4: V3-V4-V4-V5 / V3-V4-V4-V5 (46 minutes). Total difficulty (32/46)=.695
Workout 5: V3-V4-V4-V5 / V3-V4-V4-V5 (43 minutes). Total difficulty (32/43)=.744
Workout 6: V3-V4-V4-V5 / V3-V4-V4-V5 (41 minutes). Total difficulty (32/41)=.780
Workout 7: V3-V4-V4-V5 / V3-V4-V4-V5 (40 minutes). Total difficulty (32/40)=.800

Workout 8: V4-V4-V4-V5 / V4-V4-V4-V5 (42 minutes). Total difficulty (34/42)=.809

That's it. You don't even have to keep these kinds of notes - just go hard in one direction 3 weeks, then switch. Don't let yourself try to over-control this one. How many days should I train? It doesn't matter. Push yourself. How does "real" climbing fit in? Whenever and wherever you'd like. What about ARCing, and hangboarding? Don't spend too much time with the former and put the latter in with your other sessions if you'd like.

Keep it simple. Overload the system, then switch the type of overload before you go "flat."

Program 2: The Three Tier Progression (8-14 weeks, repeatable.)

This model is based on the idea that a climber's training should reflect the level at which he is performing during the season. In essence, it is a linear periodization plan, but the athlete is not subject to the plan, the plan is altered as the athlete progresses.

This entire plan usually lasts 8 to 14 weeks and can be repeated several times per season. Both the gym-based training and performance climbing at the crag will be detailed for each of the training phases.

Progression is based on completion of route redpoints. We set up a five-tier performance pyramid as an indicator of when the athlete moves on to the next phase.

The top of the pyramid is decided based on what the climber's goal route is. In the example below, let's say that route is a 13b. I will explain this as an "upside-down" pyramid, as it makes more sense with the training progression.

Tier 1: Base 1 (10 routes) 12a/b
Tier 2: Base 2 (8 routes) 12c
Tier 3: Build 1 (4 routes) 12d
Tier 4: Build 2 (2 routes) 13a
Tier 5: Performance (1-3 routes) 13b

Phase 1 - Base
This phase is characterized by a lack of focus. We concentrate on volume of total work, general strength training, and variety of "outside" training. The Base phase will last anywhere between 3 and 12 weeks, and is dependent on how much climbing you can actually get done. This program is written for climbers training indoors most of the time and climbing primarily on weekends. The primary focus of Base is to build fitness and develop redpoint mileage. Many of the routes you'll redpoint during this phase will be onsight, most should be done in two tries.

A big part of the Base phase is building volume of training; this can include several forms of workouts, from resistance training, to alpine climbing to running. You'll be taking care of *energy system development*, improving your body's ability to fuel exercise, which is not specific to movement type, but rather intensity of effort. In terms of quantifying training, your primary focus will be to increase your training duration each week, focusing more on time / volume of work than on intensity of effort. Our interest during these weeks is to build both base strength and endurance. Despite opinions to the contrary, both can be developed simultaneously, and even during the same sessions.

It is important to understand that the full-body strength, power, and endurance needs of climbers is relatively minor compared to other sports. What rock climbers need to develop are skill, coordination, finger strength, core strength, and local muscular endurance. These factors are all improved through volume of climbing.

During this phase, the performance aspect of your climbing is redpointing routes 3-5 grades below your goal performance level. These are routes that will usually be done in 1-3 tries, resulting in your ticking through your 20 (8+12) redpoints fairly quickly. Again, the duration of this phase is governed by the completion of these twenty routes. When you're done with these, you're ready to move on to the next phase: Build.

Climbing:
At the crag the plan is to redpoint 10 climbs in the *performance - (minus) 4 to 5* range, in our example, this is 12a/b. We also redpoint 8 climbs at *performance - 3* (12c). The act of redpointing is critical, so only onsight, flash, and redpoint ascents are legitimate. No toproping allowed! Any climber whose redpoint goal is 3-5 grades higher should be occasionally flashing the routes on Tier 1. At this level, many routes on the pyramid can be done each day.

It is not necessary to fully complete Tier 1 before climbing the routes of Tier 2. It is, however, necessary to complete all of the routes of Tiers 1 and 2 before moving on to Tier 3.

Training:
During this phase, the climber cycles between three workouts in the rock gym, and supplements them (if desired) with a strength program in the weight room. Our goal is to develop many facets of training at once. The climbing workouts are as follows:

Session 1: Hangboard. 3 positions (open, half-crimp, full-crimp), 5 sets each, 5 second hold. A critical note: load must be adjusted to limit hang length to 5 seconds. If you're not close to max, this is the easiest workout in the world.

Session 2: Bouldering. Sticking to short problems or sections of problems (3-8 moves), complete as many problems above your onsight-level as possible in 45 minutes. With a 15 minute warm-up this session clocks in right at an hour.

Session 3: Linked Problems. These consist of linking (or doing back-to-back without rest) two to three boulder problems for a total of 15-25 moves. The critical aspects of this workout are that movement be continuous, and that maximum recovery occur between sets. Try for 4-6 sets to begin. Advanced climbers can do up to about 10 sets per workout.

ENDURANCE
The resistance training program I recommend is pretty simple. After a good warm-up, we do 3 sets each of the following pairs:

A1: 3-5 1-arm inverted rows
A2: 3-5 1-leg squat

B1: 3-5 dumbbell bench press
B2: 2-3 deadlift

Each exercise is done to almost repetition maximum, and is done with perfect form. 2 3 days per week should do the trick.

Weak core? Then add a few sets of the following triplet:
C1: 20 Plank/Pull Combo left
C2: 10 Ankles-to-Bar
C3: 20 Plank/Pull Combo right

Phase 2 - Build
This is where we get a little more focused, and start to see performance-level efforts occasionally. During this phase, we work on extending our gained strength into strength-endurance. We start spending a lot of time with interval (anaerobic) efforts.

Now your goal is to move on to redpointing routes one to two grades easier than your goal route. Most of these routes should be similar to your end-goal route; similarities in length, angle, rock type, etc. will pay dividends.

During the build phase we drop all supplemental non-specific training. This means no more running, cycling, or random weight training. Any resistance training you do should only be done when there is no climbing option, and should consist of movements that are as sport-specific as possible, both motorically and metabolically.

The total duration of training will naturally drop off, but the intensity that you can and will train will increase. This is primarily accomplished by forced rest days before redpoint days, and by eliminating junk training. Since the routes you'll be doing have harder moves and smaller holds, the gym training you do will need to reflect this.

Climbing:
At the crag, the focus is on dispatching the routes in Tiers 3 and 4. We want to redpoint 4 routes that are two grades easier than the goal route and two routes that are one grade easier. This is a real challenge for many of our climbers, as project-level fitness is close enough that they jump the gun and start throwing themselves at a months-long effort to do one route.

Training:
In this phase, we still want to keep strength and power in mind, although the goal of the phase is to develop anaerobic endurance. To do this, we cycle between two different workouts.

Session 1: Bouldering + Hangboard. The first half of the workout (post-warm-up) is dedicated to hard bouldering. I like to see 30-45 minutes dedicated to this. You should be doing problems much harder than you can onsight, but might only get 5-8 problems in a 30 minute session. Remember that power development is your goal, not fatigue. After bouldering, rest 5-10 minutes, then move on to the hangboard. Train the same 3 positions (open, half-crimp, full-crimp) as before, 3 sets each, 8 second hold. You can add specific hang positions if necessary for your goal routes, such as tiny crimps, shallow pockets, or the like.

Session 2: Intervals. Here, we want to do either a goal-specific 4x4 session, a density bouldering session, or linked problems. We'll sometimes spend 4-6 weeks in this phase, so there is time for a progression through each of these three types of intervals. Good record keeping and clear progressions are critical - if you're anywhere near your limit, you can't mess around with wasted training sessions. I frequently dump the weight training during this phase. If you feel like you've got the juice to keep it going, stick to two days per week, same major exercises, and drop it to 2 sets per exercise. No need to go heavier on this one...we're happy just to maintain strength at this point.

Phase 3 - Performance
This is the redpoint phase. All crag days are dedicated to attempts at dispatching your

project(s). Recovery between sessions is paramount. Eat right (no trying to lose weight!), stay hydrated, and if you feel like training, do some stretching.

Climbing:
At the crag, you are redpointing. If you've done everything right, you should hit your redpoint goal fairly quickly. That's why the normal "one route at the top of the pyramid" doesn't always apply. Our experience shows that many climbers can do two to three project-level routes before fitness declines. My guess is that this is because we allow the physiological development of the athlete to determine when to change phases and not the calendar.

Training:
The only training you'll do is when you absolutely cannot get to the crag. In this case, stick to short, intense workouts. Include about 20-30 minutes of limit-level bouldering followed by 20 minutes of density bouldering or linked problems. The links should be harder than your project, but of shorter duration. If you want to do 1-2 sets of hangs on route-specific holds *at the end of a session*, you can do so.
You'll know when this phase is over. You'll be tired. Let it go. Take a couple of weeks off and then start over.

Program 3: The Non-Linear Model (infinitely repeatable)

OK, so I think we all know that a planned-out training cycle works better than pulling workouts out of your ass. A periodized plan of the classic variety can work great, but it's a little limited for many of us. Solid research shows that in sports with similar physiological demands to climbing, classic periodized plans result in better results than non-varied (just-climb-into-shape)plans.

A non-linear plan differs from a classic plan in that instead of spending several weeks focusing on one facet of training before switching to the next (i.e. hypertrophy-strength-power-endurance) the athlete switches between facets on a workout-to-workout basis. Nonlinear plans offer advantages over classic plans in some situations. For climbers looking to perform for a long trip or throughout a season, this might represent a better model. This style of plan is more flexible in how and when a peak is reached, and avoids the normal detraining pitfalls of a classic plan.

In this plan, you'll cycle through four different workouts, each of them designed as a progression from the last workout of its type. This makes for a simple-to-implement plan that allows for travel, illness, and climbing trips better than most plans. Is it the ultimate template for training? No.

Keep good records. Each of these workouts should represent a step forward from the previous one, in a 1-2-3-4-recover sequence. WTF does that mean? It means you should progress for four workouts, then back off a couple of notches, then get back after it again.

Workout 1: Hangboard + Pulls. This is a strength workout. Pick 3 hold positions (I prefer open hand, half-crimp, and full crimp) and do 4 sets each, holding each for 5-7 seconds. Load up the extra weight or hang by one hand to make this devastatingly hard. You'll want to rest for 45+ seconds between hangs, so throw in some shoulder and hip mobility work. You know you need it. After the hangboard session, do 3 sets, 3-6 reps each of inverted row, pull-up and lock, and knees-to-elbows. It's hard to load KTE well, so slow the movement down or straighten the legs to increase intensity.

Workout 2: Bouldering. This is the one you like. Boulder, but follow these rules:
  1. Change wall angles or basic hold types several times during the workout - no hanging out in the cave...
  2. Work on really hard, short problems. These things should spit you off several times.
  3. Stop when power declines. End of story. The endurance training comes later.

Workout 3: Intervals. If you've read this far, you should know what to do. For this session we look for 45-60 minutes of Problem Repeats, Linked Problems, or Traverse to Problem.

Workout 4: Long Intervals or Route Laps. This is a good place for volume climbing, ARC-style training, or technique climbing. The idea here is to work at just below threshold.

"Most people, at various points in their training careers, lose sight of the basis for all productive training. They forget that the goal is always to produce a stress that induces recovery and supercompensation, and that, as advancement continues, the increased time-frame of this response must be factored in. Variety for variety's sake is pointless. All training must be planned, and success planned for. All the variety in the world is no substitute for correct planning."
Mark Rippetoe

CLIMB
STRONG

Lap #	problems	# moves	time	success?
warm-up:				
1				
rest				
2				
rest				
3				
rest				
4				
rest				
5				
rest				
6				
rest				
7				
rest				
8				
rest				
9				
rest				
10				
rest				
11				
rest				
12				
	total time:			

the plan:
# of intervals:
rest time:
int. duration:
intensity:

notes:

54

Sample Training Sessions

These are records of actual training sessions. I have noted the training phase, goal of the session and actual session data. Please note that these are taken "out of context" but are placed here to give you some inspiration and ideas on how to build individual sessions.

Sample Session 1 – (2011-01-14)

Warm-Up:
  timed movement sets 1:1 2:2 1:1 2:2 (work:rest)

  hip + shoulder mobility 8 minutes

  hangboard - 3 rounds
    5s open hand
    30s shoulder mobility
    5s half crimp
    30s hip mobility
    5s shallow 2,3 (2,3 means middle and ring finger)
    rest 1 min

1) Traverse to Problem (20 deg. wall left to 45 deg.)
    - 15 moves to V4 reachy – success
    - 13 moves to V5 crimpy – success
    - 15 moves to V4 reachy – fail (error)
    - 13 moves to V5 crimpy – success
    - 15 moves to V4 reachy – success
    - 13 moves to V5 crimpy – success

2) Hard Reps (2 problems, one on 45 deg. wall, powerful, and one on 30 deg. wall, reachy pockets)
    - V5 – success
    - V6 – success
    - V5 – success
    - V6 – success
    - V5 – success
    - V6 – success
    - V5 – success
    - V6 – success

Sample Session 2- (2010-04-22)

Warm-Up:
    4 minutes easy climbing

    kettlebell complex – 15 min

    6 problems up to V3

1) Problems – Timed Repeats @90s
    alternating between 3 problems for 4 rounds:
    - 20 deg. crimpy V4
    - 45 deg. pockets V3
    - 45 deg. big moves V3

2) Rest 15 min – mobility

3) Rhythm Intervals – 2 rounds with 8 min between
    5 x 30sec movement / 30sec active rest
    on large edges – rest on incut big jug

4) Warm-Down – 15 min mobility + sloper hangs

This session was the second in a build where the athlete was prepping for endurance on relatively good holds.

Sample Session 3 – (2010-04-27)

Warm-Up:
    kettlebell complex – 15 min

    8 problems up to V3

1) Problems – Timed Repeats @75s
    alternating between 3 problems for 4 rounds:
    - 20 deg. crimpy V4
    - 45 deg. pockets V3
    - 45 deg. big moves V3
    (same problems as 4-22)

2) Rest 15 min – mobility

3) Rhythm Intervals – 2 rounds with 7 min between
    5 x 35sec movement / 25sec active rest
    on large edges – rest on incut big jug

4) Warm-Down – 15 min mobility + sloper hangs

This session followed #2 above. Note the shorter time interval in group 1, and the changes to group 2. The session that followed this progressed similarly, with the repeats dropping to 65 seconds, and the rest between the rhythm intervals dropping to 6 minutes.

59

ABOUT THE AUTHOR

Steve Bechtel is a coach and trainer based in Lander, Wyoming. He has been climbing for over 25 years, and has done hundred of first ascents spread across six continents. Steve holds a degree in Exercise Physiology, and is a Certified Strength and Conditioning Specialist. His facility, Elemental Performance + Fitness, is a top-level training center for climbers and other outdoor athletes.

Made in the USA
Middletown, DE
12 April 2022

64104697R00038